34880000 823356

BOOK CHARGING CARD

Accession No. _____ Call No. 978.1 NAU

Author Nault, Jennifer

Title Kansas

Date

978.1
NAU

Nault, Jennifer
Kansas

34880000 823356

KANSAS

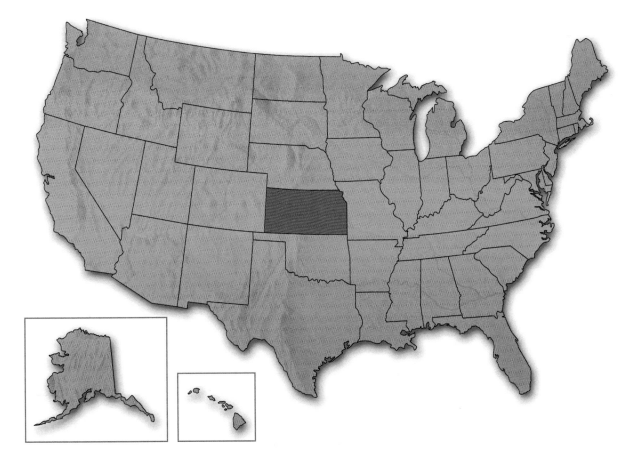

Jennifer Nault

Published by Weigl Publishers Inc.
123 South Broad Street, Box 227
Mankato, MN   56002
USA
Web site: http://www.weigl.com

Library of Congress Cataloging-in-Publication Data available upon request from the publisher. Fax: (507) 388-2746 for the attention of the Publishing Records Department.

ISBN 1-930954-90-5

Printed in the United States of America
1 2 3 4 5 6 7 8 9 10   05 04 03 02 01

Project Coordinators
Jennifer Nault
Michael Lowry
Designers
Warren Clark
Terry Paulhus
Copy Editors
Heather Kissock
Jennifer Nault
Layout
Mark Bizek
Photo Researchers
Mark Bizek
Julie Pearson

Photograph Credits
Every reasonable effort has been made to trace ownership and to obtain permission to reprint copyright material. The publishers would be pleased to have any errors or omissions brought to their attention so that they may be corrected in subsequent printings.

Cover: Wagon and Sunflowers (Michael C. Snell, Shade of the Cottonwood, L.L.C.); **Archive Photos:** pages 25, 26; **Bob Gress:** page 5; **Corbis Corporation:** pages 13, 15, 22, 24; **Corel Corporation:** pages 7, 9, 10, 11; **David E. Clouston:** pages 3, 8, 20; **Digital Vision:** page 13, **D.K. Beal:** page 27; **Evansville State Hospital:** page 11; **EyeWire:** pages 9, 14, 27; **Haskell Indian Nations University:** pages 3, 16; **Kansas Department of Transportation:** page 14; **Kansas State Historical Society:** pages 18, 19, 21; **Kansas Travel and Tourism:** pages 4, 27; **Lindsborg Chamber of Commerce:** pages 21, 22, 23; **Mark Bizek:** page 6; **Michael C. Snell / Shade of the Cottonwood, L.L.C:** pages 4, 5, 7, 8, 10, 12, 13, 14, 19, 21, 22, 29; **Monique de St. Croix:** page 24; **National Archives of Canada:** page 6; **National Freshwater Fishing Hall of Fame:** page 11; **Photodisc:** pages 15, 26; **Reynolds Alberta Museum:** page 6; **Stony Plain Records:** page 24; **Tyler Pickering:** page 28; **University of Kansas:** page 15, 16; **UT Institute of Texan Cultures at San Antonio:** page 17; **Visuals Unlimited:** page 9 (Ron Spomer); **Wakeeney Travel and Tourism:** page 25.

CONTENTS

Introduction 4

Land and Climate 8

Natural Resources 9

Plants and Animals 10

Tourism 12

Industry 13

Goods and Services 14

First Nations 16

Explorers and Missionaries 17

Early Settlers 18

Population 20

Politics and Government 21

Cultural Groups 22

Arts and Entertainment 24

Sports 26

Brain Teasers 28

For More Information 30

Glossary 31

Index 32

INTRODUCTION

When Dorothy said, "We're not in Kansas anymore, Toto," she had much to regret. The striking beauty of Kansas is not a far cry from the fictional land of Oz. The state boasts many national treasures that document its pioneer history. Kansas's charming present is closely linked to its colorful past.

Kansas is shaped by an exciting history of cowboys, outlaws, settlers, and gold prospectors. Its history has been influenced by the men and women who braved long journeys, settled, and claimed the land as their own. Kansas is still a land of opportunity, with quaint farming communities and lively urban centers.

Groups of settlers traveled across the western United States on horseback and in covered wagons called wagon trains. Two major wagon train routes crossed Kansas: the Santa Fe Trail and the Oregon Trail.

QUICK FACTS

The state capital of Kansas is Topeka, which was chosen by popular vote in 1861.

Kansas's official nickname is the "Sunflower State."

Kansas is named after the Kanza Native Americans. The word *Kanza* means "people of the south wind."

Route 66 once passed through three time zones and eight states including the southeastern corner of Kansas. Since 1985, it has been decommissioned, meaning that it is no longer in use.

Getting There

Kansas is surrounded by four states. Oklahoma lies to the south, Colorado to the west, Nebraska to the north, and Missouri to the east.

Kansas is often referred to as "America's Heartland" and "Midway U.S.A." because it lies in the geographic center of the United States mainland. It is located halfway between the east and west coasts, lying midway between Canada to the north and Mexico to the south. As well, Kansas is the **geodetic** center of North America. This means that all land surveys and maps use the state of Kansas as their midpoint.

QUICK FACTS

The state song is the popular "Home on the Range," written by Dr. Brewster Higley.

Kansas's official state amphibian is the barred tiger salamander.

Kansas entered the Union on January 29, 1861. It was the thirty-fourth state to join.

The state of Kansas is the fourteenth largest in the entire nation.

Location Map

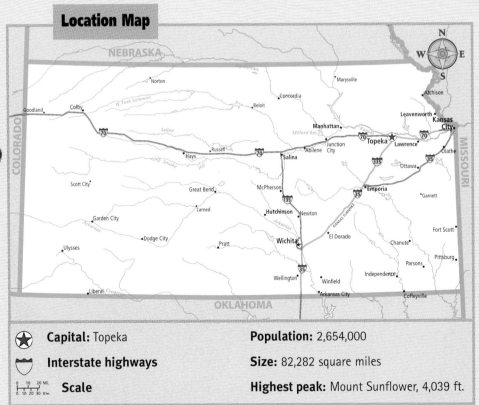

⭐ **Capital:** Topeka

🛡 **Interstate highways**

 **Scale**

Population: 2,654,000

Size: 82,282 square miles

Highest peak: Mount Sunflower, 4,039 ft.

Kansas has produced many talented people. Silent film actor "Fatty" Arbuckle, basketball player Wilt Chamberlain, United States President Dwight D. Eisenhower, and jazz musician Charlie "Yardbird" Parker have all called Kansas home.

Kansas's Amelia Earhart is known throughout the world as the first woman to fly solo across the Atlantic Ocean. Amelia Earhart is part of the state's strong presence in aviation history. Other prominent Kansas pilots include William Purvis and Charles Wilson, who almost beat the Wright brothers to the skies.

Amelia Earhart was born in 1897 in Atchinson, Kansas. She became the first female pilot to fly solo across the Atlantic Ocean in 1932.

QUICK FACTS

Kansas's state flag has a dark blue background with the state seal in the middle. The state seal displays a sunflower above a gold and blue bar that shows Kansas was a part of the **Louisiana Purchase**. The word "Kansas" appears underneath the state seal.

The city of Wichita's commitment to aviation has earned it the title, "Air Capital of the World."

KANSAS

The cottonwood is Kansas's state tree.

Kansas won an award for the most beautiful license plate in 1994. It showed Kansas's most important crop, golden waves of grain.

QUICK FACTS

Kansas's official state motto is *Ad Astra Per Aspera*, which is Latin for "To the Stars Through Difficulties."

Helium was first discovered in 1903 in Dexter, Kansas.

It was once against the law to serve ice cream on cherry pie in Kansas.

The state mammal is the American buffalo.

Horses were very important to the early Kansas settlers. They were used for transportation, industry, and recreation.

Much of the history and culture of Kansas is linked to its early settlers. Kansas was the **hub** of western frontier life, populated by **homesteaders** and outlaws. While settlers were farming and raising cattle, outlaws with names such as "Hurricane Bill" were stealing horses and robbing banks. During Kansas's colonial days, there were often clashes between Native Americans and settlers over land and resources. In more recent years, Kansas has become a place of peace and good fortune, with rolling fields of wheat and sunflowers stretching toward the sun.

Sunflower seeds are harvested for food and for the oil they contain. They are called sunflowers because they twist on their stems and follow the sun throughout the day.

LAND AND CLIMATE

Kansas has distinct natural regions that vary from flat prairies to snowcapped mountains. Desert-like plains cover the southwest region and woodlands dominate the east. Because a large sea once covered Kansas, limestone deposits are scattered throughout the state. There are also many fossil beds in Kansas, dating back millions of years. Kansas is graced by many sparkling rivers and shimmering lakes.

Ordinarily, Kansas has warm summers and cold winters. The average July temperature in Kansas is 78 °Fahrenheit, and the average January temperature is 30 °F. Temperatures do not vary much from one part of the state to the next. Greely County is the driest area in Kansas, receiving only 16 inches of **precipitation** per year. The amount of rainfall increases from west to east, peaking at 40 inches in the southeasterly corner. Kansas's skies occasionally unleash hail, blizzards, and tornadoes.

The rock formations at Mushroom Rock State Park were formed by water and wind erosion.

QUICK FACTS

The Gypsum Hills in Kansas were once called "Medicine Hills" for the river that flowed through them. Native Americans believed that the river had healing powers, and their belief was well founded. The river contains magnesium sulfate, also known as **epsom salts**, which aid human digestion.

Kansas has the largest known **meteorite** on Earth, called the *Space Wanderer*. It is located in Greensburg and contains 1,000 pounds of nickel and iron.

Gigantic cones of chalk tower over the plains at Castle Rock. Horse Thief Canyon, a tiny version of the Grand Canyon, is in the same area.

Many lakes in Kansas were once strip mines. They have since been filled with fresh water and fish.

The growing season in Kansas ranges from 150 to 200 days a year.

NATURAL RESOURCES

In spring, much of the land in Kansas is covered by fields of wheat. Most of the wheat grown in Kansas is a hardy, winter variety. It is planted in the fall and harvested in the early summer. Wheat crops account for 40 percent of the total income of all crops grown in Kansas. Wheat sales earn Kansas farmers more than $1 billion a year. This industry has earned Kansas another nickname, the "Wheat State." Other important crops in Kansas are hay, alfalfa, corn, soybeans, and sugar beets.

Kansas is rich in minerals, too. It produces large quantities of cement, stone, clay, chalk, salt, sand, zinc, and lead. Natural gas and oil are other important resources in the state. Most of Kansas's natural gas comes from a huge field in Hugoton. This reserve covers several counties in southwestern Kansas, as well as parts of Oklahoma and Texas. The state also leads the nation in the production of helium, which is **extracted** from natural gas.

There are over 130,000 tractors in Kansas.

QUICK FACTS

Kansas is about 600 miles away from any large body of water.

In 1998, more than 91 percent of the land in Kansas was used for agriculture.

Kansas wheat makes up about 20 percent of the nation's total wheat production.

Most harvested wheat is stored in concrete silos, but there are still some wooden elevators that date back to the early 1800s.

PLANTS AND ANIMALS

Kansas is a place where the deer and the antelope play, living up to the words of the state song. The open prairies provide a home for many different kinds of plants and animals. Along with frisky prairie dogs which burrow in underground homes, the prairies support coyotes, bobcats, white-tailed deer, and buffalo. Other animals that roam Kansas include beavers, raccoons, skunks, opossums, and minks.

The survival of some animals has been threatened by over-hunting. Deer had to be protected from hunters for many years because their numbers were shrinking. Today, the deer population has grown and they are no longer an **endangered** species in the state. Buffalo have not been as fortunate. The number of buffalo that once wandered the plains has decreased. They are now only found in protected parks and zoos.

Animals such as antelope and white-tailed deer are hunted in Kansas today, but the Kansas Department of Wildlife and Parks helps protect Kansas's wildlife from over-hunting.

QUICK FACTS

The Cheyenne Bottoms is a natural wetland area where millions of birds **migrate** each spring and fall. These birds include pelicans, ducks, and whooping cranes.

More than 270 species of birds visit the Quivira National Wildlife Refuge, including red-tailed hawks, bald eagles, and golden eagles.

Kansas's state bird is the western meadowlark.

Many varieties of grass spring from Kansas's soil. Buffalo grass grows in the central and western regions, while bluegrass thrives in the east. With more than 2,000 plant varieties, Kansas is home to an array of wildflowers, such as Easter daisies, asters, clover, goldenrods, morning glories, and sunflowers. In fact, millions of sunflowers bloom in Kansas's fields. Trees commonly found in the state include cottonwood, elm, oak, sycamore, ash, cedar, willow, and hickory.

It is against the law to pick wildflowers in Kansas.

QUICK FACTS

In the late 1800s, nearly 15 million sheep were brought into Kansas's central Great Plains from the Rocky Mountains.

A world record was broken in 1998 when a fisher in Kansas caught a flatheat catfish that weighed 124 pounds.

Although the **fertile** land in Kansas supports many kinds of plants, the soil is constantly threatened by erosion. The constant force of wind and water causes unprotected soil to lose moisture and nutrients. This problem has been partially solved by the improvement of farming practices and the planting of new trees.

The Kansas Champion Tree Program is dedicated to the protection and conservation of Kansas's large trees.

Fort Scott National Historic Site has twenty historic structures. The exteriors of the buildings have been restored to their original 1840s appearance.

TOURISM

Several interesting sites in Kansas offer reminders of its early pioneer history. On the Santa Fe Trail, visitors can still find ruts made by wagons more than 100 years ago. Kansas is well known for its cattle drives, gunfighters, and dusty prairie towns. Visitors to Dodge City can ramble around Boot Hill Cemetery, the location of a **legendary** gunfight. The name, "Boot Hill," comes from the tale of a gunman who was killed and buried on the side of the hill with his boots still on. Many other historic forts remain open to the public. Fort Larned and Fort Scott have been restored, allowing visitors a chance to experience the history of the American Civil War.

Kansas has more than 150 lakes and 24 state parks. These parks include natural areas that are open to fishers, boaters, swimmers, and hikers. Another great way for tourists to appreciate the outdoors is on horseback. Trail rides through the sloping flint hills near Eureka allow guests to roam the land as early pioneers did.

Although not an official Dodge City cemetery, people who had no money and no family in the area were buried at Boot Hill Cemetery.

QUICK FACTS

Dodge City is the second windiest city in the United States.

Tourists may visit Cawker to see the world's largest ball of twine. It is forty feet tall and weighs 17,000 pounds.

Abilene, Baldwin City, and Dodge City have restored passenger trains for visitors to ride.

The Stearman biplane was produced by Boeing in Wichita.

INDUSTRY

Kansas ranks high in the nation in manufacturing. The state makes items such as camping gear, heating and air-conditioning equipment, snowmobiles, and airplanes. The state has about eighty different aircraft companies, including Boeing and Cessna. More than 266,000 aircraft have been made in Kansas. Other products manufactured in Kansas are tires, paint, chemicals, industrial machinery, rubber, greeting cards, and clothing. Wichita and Kansas City are the state's main manufacturing centers.

Service industries have replaced agriculture as Kansas's largest economic asset. Still, many service industries revolve around agricultural products. For instance, many people work in the sale and transport of raw products such as wheat, hay, and alfalfa.

QUICK FACTS

Aviation plays a leading role in the state's economy. Kansas produces about 60 percent of the nation's general aviation aircraft.

Big Brutus, the world's biggest coal shovel, is 160 feet tall. Big Brutus is taller than a fifteen-story building.

In 1915, an oil discovery close to El Dorado created an oil **boom.**

About 185,000 people are employed in Kansas's manufacturing industry.

GOODS AND SERVICES

Kansas is a leader in transportation as a result of its central location. Since its early days, Kansas has played an important role in the movement of consumer goods across the country. Roads provide the nation with access to the state's wealth of agricultural products. Its extensive highway system makes Kansas one of the nation's top states for total area covered by highways. Kansas also imports and exports by air, rail, and water, via barges on the Missouri River. The transportation industry employs more Kansans than any other industry.

The trucking industry in Kansas delivers goods to the residential areas of the state and helps support the oil and gas, agriculture, and meat packing industries.

QUICK FACTS

The first newspaper in Kansas was the *Shawnee Sun*, printed in the Shawnee language. Jotham Meeker, a missionary, published it in 1834.

The state's busiest airport is in Wichita.

Kansas has about 133,000 miles of roads and highways.

With so many roads, many Kansans work in road maintenance.

Many Hollywood movies have been filmed in Kansas, including the 1996 movie *Mars Attacks!* and *Paper Moon* in 1973.

In 1861, Dr. Erastus Wolcott performed the world's first successful kidney removal in Milwaukee.

The Kansas State University College of Veterinary Medicine uses waterbeds to support horses during operations.

Many Kansans work in retail industries, such as automobile dealerships, grocery and department stores, and restaurants. Other people work in private hospitals, law firms, and hotels.

It is not difficult to access current information in the state. Residents are given much to read, hear, watch, and learn. The communication services in Kansas include many newspapers and radio and television stations. Kansas has 265 different newspapers, 175 radio stations, and 20 television stations. The state has six state universities, including one of the country's leading agricultural colleges at Kansas State University.

There is plenty of shopping in Wichita's downtown area, with over 300 merchants in the historic Delano shopping district.

A council of forty-four chiefs and seven military societies governed the ten major bands of the Cheyenne.

FIRST NATIONS

Kansas had a very **diverse** population of Native Peoples when Europeans first arrived in the area. Some of the Native Peoples living in Kansas included the Cheyenne, Pawnee, Osage, Kiowa, Kansa (Kaw), Wichita, and Arapaho. The earliest people in Kansas hunted buffalo and grew beans, corn, and squash.

Several new groups of Native Americans entered Kansas from the east after 1830. They moved into the region because European settlers were moving westward, pushing Native Peoples off their land. The United States Congress passed a law that forced Native Americans to move west of the Mississippi River. Kansas became their new home. At the time, most Native Americans had little say over where they could live.

Today, there are three **reservations** in northeast Kansas. The Haskell Indian Nations University educates students from more than 120 different Native American groups. In the summer, Native Americans from across North America meet in Kansas for **powwows**, which feature dancing and singing. Many Native Peoples attend powwows to renew old traditions and preserve their rich heritage.

The modern powwow is based on the common values of all Native Americans: honor, respect, tradition, and generosity.

Francisco Vasquez de Coronado was the first explorer to visit southwestern North America.

EXPLORERS AND MISSIONARIES

Spanish explorer Francisco Vasquez de Coronado was the first European to set foot in Kansas in 1541. He traveled from Mexico across the Pecos River searching for a place called Quivira. A Native-American guide had told Coronado that a lost city called Quivira was rich in gold. Although they searched, the explorers never found gold, and they left soon after.

Juan de Padillo was a priest on Coronado's **expedition**. He returned to Kansas in 1542, hoping to bring **Christianity** to the Native Americans. He founded the first mission in the area, north of present-day Wichita. Soon after, Father Padillo was killed because of his beliefs.

In 1682, the French explorer René-Robert Cavelier claimed Kansas for Louis XIV, the King of France.

Juan de Padillo became the first Christian **martyr** in the United States. There is a monument to him in Herington, Kansas.

EARLY SETTLERS

The United States government encouraged early settlers to move to Kansas. It allowed them to buy land, although Native Peoples were living there at the time. The government further encouraged settlement by refusing to force settlers off land when Native Peoples protested. Soon, the number of settlers moving to Kansas rapidly increased.

Many people of European **ancestry** sailed to the United States. They came to Kansas looking for jobs, free land, and a little adventure. The Mennonite pioneers from Russia were among the first groups to settle in Kansas. They belonged to a **devout** religious group that followed a simple lifestyle of hard work and regular worship. Many Mennonites came to Pennsylvania in the early 1700s to gain religious freedom. Later, they spread to Kansas and other midwestern states.

Mennonites are known for their modest clothing and simple way of life.

QUICK FACTS

Rifles were smuggled into Kansas during the American Civil War. They were transported in boxes marked "Bibles."

People called Kansas the "Breadbasket of America" when wheat became its leading crop in 1894.

Walls in sod houses were made of strips of packed dirt laid horizontally like bricks.

QUICK FACTS

Laura Ingalls Wilder, whose first book was *Little House in the Big Woods,* traveled in a covered wagon through Kansas. She stayed there a short time before finally settling in Wisconsin.

Mennonites strongly believed in the importance of reasoning and thinking. Many of them became writers and artists.

Early settlers made butter turn yellow by squeezing carrot gratings and warm milk through fabric.

Mennonites followed the teachings of the Bible carefully. They did not believe in fighting wars or holding positions that required the use of force. In 1874, Mennonites brought Turkey Red winter wheat to Kansas. This sturdy variety of wheat suited the climate in Kansas and helped give the state an edge in agriculture. The Turkey Red variety of wheat has become an important crop for many Kansas farmers. Today, Mennonites are successful farmers who usually live in their own tiny communities where their religion is practiced and preserved. Many farmers in Kansas have Mennonites to thank for their hardy wheat crops.

Mennonites can depend on the members of their community for help in anything they do. They strongly believe in the importance of a caring community.

German settlers moved to Kansas in its early days.

POPULATION

Cowboys make up a segment of Kansas's population.

Kansas has a small population, of 2.6 million residents. It is split into 105 separate counties. Of the total population, nearly 13 percent live in Wichita. Although Topeka is the state capital, its population ranks third in the state. Following Wichita, Kansas City, and Topeka, the next largest cities are Overland Park, Lawrence, and Olathe.

Very few people have moved to Kansas from other countries. Most of the early settlers who arrived in Kansas came from New England. These settlers were of European ancestry. New England settlers were followed by a small wave of immigrants from Europe. Most came from Germany, Scandinavia, Russia, and Great Britain. People born in other countries make up only 2 percent of the state's population, with people of German ancestry making up the largest portion. About 5 percent of Kansas's total population is African American.

QUICK FACTS

About 22,000 Native Americans live in Kansas.

The largest city in Kansas is Wichita. It has over 330,000 residents.

None of the state's major cities are in the west. In fact, Garden City ranks highest in the west with only 25,000 people.

Very few Kansans drop out of high school. An amazing 89 percent of the state's residents have a high school diploma.

There are over 660,000 family households in Kansas.

Although Susan Salter was nominated for mayor as a joke, she became the mayor of Argonia with two-thirds of the vote.

A Kansas woman was the first female to serve as Treasurer of the United States. President Harry Truman appointed Georgia Neese Clark Gray as Treasurer in 1949.

The thirty-fourth president of the United States was from Kansas. Dwight D. Eisenhower grew up in Abilene and was elected twice, in 1952 and 1956.

Kansas's constitution has been in use since 1859.

POLITICS AND GOVERNMENT

Kansas has taken many steps toward bringing equality to its citizens. In 1954, the state was the first in the nation to ban **segregation** in schools, allowing children of all races to learn together. This court decision encouraged governments in other states to follow suit. As a result, segregation in schools in the United States was eventually brought to a halt.

Kansas has also led the nation in its treatment of women. The state granted women the right to own property and ownership of their children in 1861. In 1887, women were given the right to vote in city elections. The same year that women gained the right to vote, Kansas elected the first female mayor in the United States. Susan Salter became mayor of Argonia.

Kansas has three branches of government: executive, legislative, and judicial. The executive is led by the state governor. This branch decides how to spend state money. The legislative branch is made up of a 40-member Senate and a 125-member House of Representatives and is responsible for making the laws. Lastly, the judicial branch ensures laws are followed and governs the state's courts.

Suffragettes from Kansas helped women in the United States gain the right to vote in state and national elections.

CULTURAL GROUPS

Most early settlers to Kansas had already been living in the United States, but were of European descent. Many still celebrate their cultural traditions at festivals throughout the state.

The first Swedish pioneers settled in the Smokey Valley in 1868. They were attracted to Kansas by the prospect of free land and jobs laying railroad track. They faced hardships when they first moved to the area. Along with other farmers in the Smokey Valley region, they faced droughts, heat waves, and plagues of grasshoppers while trying to establish their farms. Still, many Swedish trailblazers were successful in settling the land.

Diners can go to Lindsborg to enjoy an authentic Swedish Smorgasbord.

QUICK FACTS

Many Scottish people settled in mining communities in the southeastern part of Kansas.

A popular event at the *Svensk Hyllningsfest* festival is the Swedish Smorgasbord. This feast includes such Scandinavian foods as meatballs, potato sausage, deviled eggs, and smoked salmon.

Many people of Swedish descent live in Lindsborg, also known as "Little Sweden." The city of Lindsborg has several festivals that feature some of the Swedish traditions of its citizens. *Svensk Hyllningsfest* is a festival that features traditional Swedish costumes and food, folk dances, and a lively parade. The first *Svensk Hyllningsfest* was thought to have started as a celebration of the landing of Swedes in America. Many Kansans enjoy learning about Swedish traditions and sampling their tasty food.

Svensk Hyllningfest takes place in October in odd-numbered years only.

Viking history is an important aspect of Swedish culture.

Rodeos are a popular form of entertainment in Kansas.

ARTS AND ENTERTAINMENT

Kansas's flourishing arts and entertainment scene is its best kept secret. In the heart of cowboy country, Kansas is rodeo territory. Many rodeos are held in Kansas during the late spring and continue until early fall. People can watch cowboys calf roping, bull riding, and barrel racing. Brave spectators can enter cow chip throwing events, which involve throwing dried cow dung as far as they can.

Kansas also has many theaters, museums, fairs, and music festivals. The state is known for its summer jazz and **bluegrass** festivals. People can attend bluegrass performances, which feature this form of traditional country music. Banjos are unique to bluegrass music, and are usually played in an unusual, three-finger style. Also, no bluegrass band would be complete without the mandolin and the fiddle. Attending a lively bluegrass festival will get even the most shy person square dancing.

Kansas has a rich jazz heritage. Jazz festivals are held in Overland Park and Manhattan.

Kirstie Alley has received many awards for her work on the television show *Cheers*.

Many well-known writers and poets come from Kansas. Langston Hughes, who is a highly respected poet, wrote about the African-American experience in the United States. Kansan Damon Runyon wrote the hit musical *Guys and Dolls*.

Kansas has also produced some famous Hollywood actors and actresses. Kirstie Alley, Edward Asner, Dennis Hopper, and Don Johnson all hail from the Sunflower State. Hattie McDaniel was a famous actress born in Wichita in 1895. She was the first African American to win an Academy award. She won the Best Supporting Actress Oscar for her role as Mammy in the movie *Gone With the Wind*.

Quick Facts

The Sedgwick County Zoo in Wichita has about 2,500 animals and an indoor rain forest.

Christmas is a special time of year for many Kansas residents. There are amazing Christmas displays during this holiday season. The town of WaKeeney is known as "the Christmas City of the High Plains" for its 40-foot Christmas tree covered in more than 6,000 lights.

Don Johnson (right) graduated from a Wichita high school in 1967.

Running clubs are a popular way for Kansans to enjoy the great outdoors.

SPORTS

While Kansas has no major professional sports teams, its many parks and recreational areas offer plenty of outdoor activities for the sports enthusiast.

Kansas has gained popularity among fishers for its many lakes. The state's fishing season is open year round, drawing fishers to cast their rods in Kansas's waters when the fishing season in their home state is over.

Kansas has many trails for those who enjoy adventure. Horseback riders, walkers, runners, and cyclists all share these trails. Many trails in Kansas are characterized by sharp twists and turns.

QUICK FACTS

Kansas resident Glen Cunningham held the world record in the one-mile run during the 1930s.

Wilt "The Stilt" Chamberlain played basketball for the Kansas Jayhawks in 1957 and 1958. He also earned recognition in track and field during these years.

Kansas has many natural parks for nature lovers to enjoy. People in the state can experience the fresh air and beautiful scenery of Kansas in a variety of ways. Among some of the activities available to residents and visitors alike are camping, biking, boating, and water sports.

With such a large number of wildflowers, some people enjoy going on wildflower tours—spotting, identifying, and photographing the beautiful flowers native to Kansas.

QUICK FACTS

In 1988, Wilt Chamberlain returned to Kansas to have his jersey officially retired.

Every summer, Kansas hosts a biking competition called the "Death Ride." Bikers ride 62 miles through heat, hills, and Native American burial sites.

Water sports such as boating and water skiing are popular recreational activities in Kansas.

Brain Teasers

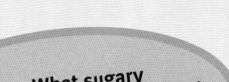

1 What sugary snack was invented in Kansas?

Answer: The O'Henry! candy bar was invented by Tom Henry in Arkansas City.

2 Who was the legendary lawman who kept the peace in Abilene until he was fired for shooting at a group of rowdy cowboys and killing one of his own policemen?

Answer: Wild Bill Hickock. He kept the lawless town of Abilene under control in 1871.

3 What is Hutchinson, Kansas famous for?

Answer: Hutchinson, Kansas has the largest salt deposit in the world. The Hutchinson salt deposit produces more than 44 million tons of salt every year.

4 Who invented the first patented helicopter?

Answer: William Purvis and Charles Wilson of Goodland, Kansas. In 1909, the helicopter was completed.

5

Who was Carry A. Nation and what is she famous for?

Answer: Carry A. Nation was a woman who decided to put an end to saloons that were illegally selling alcohol. She became famous after smashing various saloons with a hatchet.

6

How is the word Jayhawk connected to Kansas?

Answer: The Jayhawk was a mythical bird of Ireland that preyed upon other birds. During the American Civil War, people who roamed the plains were called Jayhawkers. They were thought to have begged and borrowed their way across the state.

7

Why was Kansas known as "Bleeding Kansas?"

Answer: This name was earned when battles broke out between anti-slavery and pro-slavery groups in 1856. More than fifty people were killed in these battles.

8

What was the Dust Bowl?

Answer: The name "Dust Bowl" refers to the region where a terrible drought struck in the early 1930s. The region included Kansas, Colorado, Texas, and Oklahoma.

FOR MORE INFORMATION

Books

Fradin, Dennis. *Kansas: In Words and Pictures*. New York: Children's Press, 1980.

Ise, John. *Sod and Stubble: The Story of a Kansas Homestead*. Nebraska: University of Nebraska Press, 1967.

Kent, Zachary. *America the Beautiful: Kansas*. New York: Children's Press, 1990.

Web sites

You can also go online and have a look at the following Web sites:

Kansas Information Network
http://www.state.ks.us

Kansas State History Society
http://www.kshs.org

Stately Knowledge, Kansas
http://www.ipl.org/youth/stateknow/ks1.html

Some Web sites stay current longer than others. To find other Kansas Web sites, enter search terms, such as "Kansas," "bluegrass," "Sunflower State," or any other topic you want to research.

GLOSSARY

ancestry: past relatives

bluegrass: a style of music that is similar to country western music

boom: period of rapid economic growth and prosperity

Christianity: Western religion based on the belief that Jesus Christ lived and was the son of God.

devout: devotion to religious beliefs or activities

diverse: different or varied

endangered: any species of life that is threatened with extinction

epsom salts: a white salt that is used in medicine

erosion: the wearing away of rock and soil

expedition: the group of people and ships that make a journey

extracted: something that is obtained through a chemical process

fertile: productive land that can support abundant plant growth

geodetic: the center point of a land mass

homesteaders: people who moved and settled in new areas

hub: center or focal point

legendary: a story or a well known character that is ungrounded in history

Louisiana Purchase: a vast amount of land that was purchased by the United States from France in 1803

martyr: a person who suffers or dies for the sake of her or his beliefs

meteorite: a mass of stone or metal that has fallen to the earth from outer space

migrate: to move from one region to another

powwow: a Native American ceremony

precipitation: rain, sleet, snow, or hail

reservation: an area of land reserved for Native Americans

segregation: the regulated separation of people of different races

suffragettes: women who fought for women's rights, including the right to vote

INDEX

Abilene 12, 21, 28
agriculture 9, 13, 14, 19
aviation 6, 13

Big Brutus 13
bluegrass 24, 30, 31
Boot Hill Cemetery 12

Cavalier, Rene-Robert 17
Chamberlain, Wilt 6, 26, 27
Cheyenne Bottoms 10
Civil War 12, 18, 24, 29
Clark, William 17
de Coronado, Francisco Vasquez 17
cottonwood 6, 11
cowboys 4, 20, 24, 28

Dodge City 12

Earhart, Amelia 6
Eisenhower, Dwight D. 6, 21

farming 4, 7, 11
gold prospectors 4
grain 6
Gray, Georgia Neese Clark 21

helium 7, 9
Hickock, Wild Bill 28

Kanza 4

Lewis, Meriwether 17
limestone 8
Louisiana Purchase 6, 17, 31

manufacturing 13, 14
McDaniel, Hattie 25
Mennonite 18, 19
meteorite 8, 31
Missouri River 14, 17

Nation, Carry A. 29
Native Americans 4, 7, 8, 16, 17, 18, 20, 27

Oregon Trail 4

de Padillo, Juan 17
pioneers 12, 18, 22
Purvis, William 6, 28

Quivira National Wildlife Refuge 10

rodeo 20, 24
Runyon, Damon 25

Salter, Susan 21
Santa Fe Trail 4, 12
sunflowers 4, 6, 7, 11
Svensk Hyllningsfest 23

Topeka 4, 5, 20
transportation industry 14

wheat 7, 9, 13, 18, 19
Wichita (city) 6, 13, 14, 15, 17, 20, 25
Wilson, Charles 6, 28
Wolcott, Dr. Erastus 15